Table of Contents

Helpful Links

The Path To Freedom

The Path
To
Freedom

▶ **HOW TO CREATE A COMMUNITY OF LIKE-MINDED AND DEDICATED FANS WHO WILL PURCHASE ANYTHING FROM YOU**

DANIEL MAC SWEENEY

For my Family -

EDDIE, KATHERINE, STACEY & EDWARD MAC SWEENEY,
who taught me the value of life itself. Work hard and you shall achieve what you want
and what you aim for. I love you all like there's no tomorrow.

My Family -

SINEAD my wife and our daughter CAOIMHE, who I will always love and care for until
the end of time. Without you, I would not have achieved what I have, because
everything I do, I do for you.

Table of Contents

Copyright

ISBN 978-1-387-67416-9 paperback

Dedication

They say you learn from life's experiences but I think that you learn from who you know. I would not have written this book if it wasn't for my parents, the ones who created me, raised me with good values, worked extremely hard to provide for my siblings and me, who struggled to give us the best childhoods any child could ask for. Thank you, Mom and Dad- you are my heroes.

I want to thank my grandparents. They taught me the value of hard work and entrepreneurship as they were all business people themselves; a farmer, an egg seller and sweet shop owners. I love you all, my thoughts and prayers are always with you... My wife. I love you with all my heart, without you this book would have taken years. You kept believing in me when I struggled to believe in myself. I did this for you and our daughter. You are my rock and my best friend. Thank you to our daughter, who taught me things that only teenagers know and for letting me finish my work in peace.

To my sister, who listened to me when I wanted to clear my head of Entrepreneurial thoughts. This made a big difference to me as talking and training with you helped me leaps and bounds. And to my younger brother who I competed with to better myself, unknowingly to him.

I want to thank my mentors who taught me things that would have otherwise taken years for me to understand or figure out. You have been like teachers to me, some of you don't know who I am but I strive to be better because of you.

The fffers from my community Financial Freedom Forever. You are what drove me daily. Without you I'd be sharing content to no one but myself. Thank you for encouraging me everyday and becoming my friends. I believe that through this book, I can give back and provide you with the knowledge to succeed like I have.
Thank you.

Daniel Mac Sweeney

About Me

At this very moment, I'm writing the first few lines of my book but that's not the only thing I'm doing right now, I'm also working. I work in a factory that makes windows & doors for houses. I do shift work in my job which means I work nights one week & days the next with 12-hour shifts three to four days a week. I like my job even though it can be very long and boring but it gives me time to listen to motivational podcasts and read inspirational books on my phone. This is not the type of work I wanted to end up doing in my life but the one I had arrived at.

When I was young I taught I was set to do great things. I wanted to become a leader, a spaceman, a fireman or an explorer and to save people that needed to be saved. As a young boy, I'd always been adventurous. I drove my mother crazy because I used to go missing all the time. I'd constantly search out new places and make new friends. When I think back to my youth I wonder when I first started showing signs of entrepreneurship and leadership.

This brings me back to when I was between 8 and 12 years old. I was a leader and kids used to look up to me. I'd be able to tell others my age and younger what to do, when to do it and how to do it. I knew then that I was in charge and knew how to win so I started a little group. We built bases and battled our rivals in a field below my grandparents sweet shop. There was a forest near the field where we would conduct training exercises and come up with a game plan on how to defeat our rivals. While leader of this group I started to show some entrepreneurial traits and brought in kids to join who all had their own individual skills and knowledge to benefit the group. I had a strong kid, a clever one, a builder, one who could speak another language and then there was me, the leader who could direct and manage situations.

I learnt a lot back then on how to be a leader, however, as I moved onto secondary school things started to go wrong for me. I started following someone else.

In my second year of secondary school I made a friend who I followed and listened to but he soon started to manipulate me and others with his words. This "so-called friend" turned a lot of people in my year against me. He said venomous words to them, that were really his own words and pretended that I was the one saying horrible things about them. I was then subjected to have a fight with another pupil at break time but instead of fighting I walked away from it upset and humiliated. It felt like the whole school was there to watch this and beat me up physically and mentally. This crowd of teenagers called me terrible names and threatened to beat me up the minute the fight was meant to start. It was a horrible situation to find myself in. After walking away I walked to my grandparents house and told my mother, who then brought me to see the principal, who suspended all the pupils that were involved in bullying me. Over the following two years I put all my energy into building up my reputation and my mind. I would never again let an individual bully me and be subjected to such humiliation.

I feel that this particular experience taught me so much about myself and others. Now I make sure that I stand up for myself and keep striving to improve myself daily. In part this has made me into the person I am today.

Business was in my blood as all my grandparents ran their own businesses. My fathers parents were farmers and worked off the land while also buying and selling animals. They had a hen house and my grandmother would call from house to house selling her hen's eggs. After my great grandfather retired from being the local shoemaker my mothers parents opened a sweet shop after getting married. They set up shop in his house in the local town and were very successful until they retired in the late 90's. Up to this day I still get asked when "Sheahan's sweet shop" is opening again? This shows the reputation and popularity they had built up in the town and people far and wide still reminisce about their childhood in this shop. I spent most of my time growing up in this sweet shop and can say that these were some of the best years of my life. Going to the wholesale shop to buy products with my mother, wrapping sweets, stocking shelves and serving the customers was a fantastic experience for any child.

I think one of the reasons I didn't made an effort until recent years is that I expected it to happen for me, a business landing on my lap, so to speak. I probably thought deep down that I would automatically become successful by not having to do much at all. This was the wrong mindset to have. I realise now that to be successful takes hard work, focus, determination and a clear idea of what you want to achieve. Being a natural optimist I can always see good things happening and the good in others. I believe in visualising your goals and the expected results and outcome and can see myself on top of the world in the near future, traveling the world and being free from financial restraints.

Not long after leaving school I got a job in the local Cinema. I had always loved movies and the alternative world they provided you with. During this time I got to see most of the big blockbusters before anyone else. I went from working as a shop assistant to a box-office assistant to being a projectionist. This was my favourite place to work as a worker, I felt part of a team and the people I worked alongside became my second family. This job also enabled me to do one of my favourite things, watch movies for free. The cinema owners taught me many valuable lessons, such as how to stand back from confrontation from irate customers, to working together as a team to achieve tasks efficiently and effectively and to have complete control of a situation if an issue arose.

During my time working in the cinema and the jobs after I wasted a lot of time and money on drinking and partying when I could have been educating myself and starting my business earlier on. At the time I was more interested in girls, drinking and having fun. Don't get me wrong, those things are very important too, you have to have fun and experience all of the things that come with this. It's fine to let loose but doesn't make the same mistake I made. Skill up while you're having fun!

I was now 25 and my brother, a cousin, his friend and I decided to go to Australia with a view to travelling, working and living in the sun for the next two years. Both my brother and cousin were qualified carpenters after just finishing college, his friend was a teacher and I was just a simple worker with no visible skill, trade or degree.We travelled Australia from north to south doing all the things you'd expect to do in Australia. Bungee jumping, sky diving, snorkelling out on the Great Barrier Reef, driving the great ocean road, camping on Fraser Island and jumping waves on Bondi Beach. We drove everywhere in an old transit van camper which we bought along the way. After two months of travelling we arrived in Melbourne, a city with over 5 million people, more people than the whole of Ireland.
 The two boys got jobs right away with their carpentry qualifications. My cousin's friend stayed in Brisbane travelling because she was going back to Ireland and I spent my time on the computer looking for a job. I was almost broke and was down to my last $1,000 so when I finally got a job with a Seo web developer business I was delighted. After meeting with the boss I pretty much got hired on the spot because he liked my attitude and manner. My boss and the company owner said I had a great voice for the phone. I thought, "Jesus, I must be ugly!". He had a similar story to mine having wasted time drinking and messing around, feeling depressed until he had an epiphany. An "Aha moment!" in which he had the courage to start his own business after upskilling and educating himself on design and SEO.

 I was hired as a cold caller which involved setting up meetings between my boss and potential clients. As this was a new position I helped write copy for the script that would be used for making phone calls and reaching out to potential clients. As you can imagine, I was very nervous at first and was shocked at the abuse I received from people over the phone who thought I was trying to scam them. Eventually, as I got into it I was setting up two to three meetings a day. My past helped me overcome the abuse I encountered daily from people that had no interest and as I called more people I developed different tactics on how to swing a conversation and organise that all important meeting.

 If you travel to Australia on a holiday working visa for a year, you have to gain sponsorship or work three months on a farm, fruit picking or dairy farming to stay for a second year.
 So two months after starting my new job, I left to go fruit picking in order to get my second-year visa. Another of my cousins arrived over from Germany and I convinced her to go fruit picking with me straight away to get it over and done with so she could enjoy her time living in a city afterwards.

It's hard for me to describe how bad this experience was but believe me when I say it was "three months of living hell". We lived in tents which were roasting hot everyday with no air-con and it was 40 degrees Celsius for a few days and a constant 30 thereafter. (104 Fahrenheit for you Americans) There were flies everywhere, constant noise from others and our surroundings and just a really unhealthy environment to be in. I certainly hadn't given my cousin the best first experience of Australia! For those three months we lived off of fruit, vegetables and bags of wine known locally as 'Goon'. I'll never forget one week when I didn't get paid because something went wrong with the bank. I checked my account and there was less than $100 left in my account. I had never been this broke in my working life and swore that I would never again be. After a gruelling few months, I moved back to Melbourne, walked on to a building site and asked for a job. I got it and worked hard six days a week to climb out of the poverty I had put myself in. My father travelled over to see how my brother and I were doing and spent a month convincing me to return home to Ireland.

Eventually that's what I did. But struggling in Australia wasn't the only reason I wanted to go home, that year my Grandfather of the same name passed away. I still had three grandparents left and I wanted to go home to spend as much time with them as possible. I knew I was very lucky to have them alive so intended on making the most out of this. Over the next two years two more of my Grandparents passed away so I was happy with my decision to move home in that I had spent valuable time with them. Once home I got a job in a local supermarket as a deli assistant and took up running to keep myself busy and get fit.

Starting a business still had not entered my mind. I got an iPhone 3 and loved the way I could basically carry my computer around with me in my pocket at all times. After having spent a few months improving my running I started doing races. I did 5ks, 10ks, Adventure races and a duathlon. At the time I was also reading a book called "The Four Hour Work Week" by Tim Ferris and a post on the same named website "How to Start an App Empire", both of which got me thinking about creating my own App. I spent my time researching and designing an App for running since this was what I was interested in and was determined to build an App to make it easy for people to find races within Ireland.

Since starting to compete in a variety of races I realised how difficult it was to actually find out where the next one was happening. I thought that's what I need to do, put all the upcoming races in one place for people. I searched for developers on Elance (now UpWork) and found one that suited my budget. After further tweaking and design changes I had my App designed and finalised ready for the App Store three months later. It cost me $5,500 in total to make and I spent another $1,500 on updates, business cards, signs and posters.

What I hadn't done was set aside a budget for advertising and a website.
The App was free for people to download and use but without any marketing and anyone knowing about it I had no downloads. For nearly a year I continued to try to grow the App and get people to use it. But as I had to keep filling up the database myself, it took up too much of my time, money and effort so I had to shut it down. I had experienced my first failure. This was very disappointing for me as I had put in a lot of work to the App but had missed out on the 'all important' factors needed for developing a business.

What lessons did I learn?

• I rushed in too quickly
• I had no fans set up before developing the App
• I had no website to promote my App
• I listened to the wrong people and bought things I didn't need

During this disappointment also came one of the greatest highlights of my life so far, I met the girl of my dreams. She started working in the same place as me soon after I did. Within six months we were head over heels about each other and in the third week of dating, we moved in together and never looked back. We have since married and she has been a driving factor in my success always believing in me and encouraging me to be better.
Even though my App had failed I now had even more of an urge to make something of myself.

It was New Year's night when we were hanging out wearing the onesies that she got us for Christmas when we came up with the idea for my next venture "Original Onesies". I found a website online called Alibaba. I spent some time on this site and found a supplier that sold onesies and ordered over 110 to test the business pretty quickly after coming up with the idea. With this order I got 10 free onesies having spent $1,000 on the onesies which worked out at around $9.09 each.
I intended on selling them according to size. The cost would be $40 with shipping for adults and $29.99 with shipping for children. Profit-wise I was looking at making around $25 from the adults and $17 from the kids onesies. I made a few sales in the first month selling 15 onesies on the website and 5 through the Facebook page. But before I was able to even get those sales I had to find out how to build a website. I found someone on Elance to create a Wordpress website for me for $100 and within a few weeks I had modified the website myself using ideas and examples from the backend of the site that was made for me. Since I had some experience of Seo from my time in Australia, I used some of the techniques that I had learned to bring it to rank on the top 20 pages on Google using certain keywords.

While working on this, I did a popular 120km cycle called the 'Ring of Kerry charity cycle', alongside my girlfriend and over 10,000 other cyclists. During it, we took a rest break and stopped at a stunning Kerry beach. Even with thousands of people cycling by us, it felt like we were the only two in the world and I popped the Question and she said "Yes!". I was thrilled. However, a few days later, the Onesie supplier I was dealing with went bankrupt and shut down and because I now had no supplier I had to shut Original Onesies down until I found a new one. Other life factors and interests came in the way after this and I didn't reopen the store again until this year, 2017.

My wife and I got married on the 2nd of January 2016 which was one of the happiest days of my life. My wife had a daughter, whom I call my own and these two girls are now my life and I would do just about anything for them. Now even more than ever I was focused on being a success, a business leader and an entrepreneur.

I now had two failures behind me, the App and the Onesies, both of which taught me huge lessons about the world of entrepreneurship. Soon after completing the charity cycle I found and became interested in Domain names. For those of you who don't know, a Domain name is a unique name that identifies a website and costs money to purchase, the better the name the higher the cost. For example, Facebook.com is a domain name and all the profiles and pages are connected to that name.
You can forward names to your main domain names page like Facebook have done with FB.com.

Domains are a type of virtual property. You can make up a name which you can purchase from as little as $.99 to names in the low thousands. If you want a specific name, that is owned already, it can cost you a lot, depending on what the name is. Facebook bought FB.com for $8,500,000 in 2010. After learning how much could be made from domains, I was sucked in. It took me a few months to figure out what was worth money and what cost money. I joined a Forum called Namepros. Here I connected with like-minded people, learned what sold and why, the tools to use, the marketplaces that worked best and tips and tricks these domainers used to buy and sell their domains. I was hooked and started buying names that were growing in popularity and selling them for a few hundred $$$ at a time. I created my own portfolio website to showcase my domains and built a website to talk about domain names. I also wrote two eBooks to educate people on Domain names so that they could get off to a great start in the domaining world just as I had after self educating.

Over the years I have put all my time and energy into learning how to build websites, drive SEO, promote affiliate links, domain names, eBooks, products and marketing. My goal is to teach you what I've learned, the skills I have gained and the mistakes I've made so that you won't make the same ones. And most importantly I will teach you how to succeed in your own business.

Through this book, I want to be completely honest with you and show you what works

and what doesn't.
 I am not super rich just yet. I am not Gary Vaynerchuk or Tony Robbins what I am is just like you.

 I have the determination that you have now and the knowledge to pass on to you. That is why you are here reading this right now. You want to change your life, you want to be a success and you want to do this for you! You no longer want to put all your hard work into someone else's business when you could be putting this into your own. Now is your time. It doesn't matter if you want huge success like the above-mentioned entrepreneurs or to gain small successes. I am going to show you the way in the following chapters...

 It's down to you to work hard, listen and understand why you're doing this.
 You are probably asking why should I listen to you.
 Because as you read this book you will be following the steps I took to achieve my own success alongside your own journey. I made change happen in my life and you can do exactly the same.

 As Social Media Guru, Gary Vaynerchuk says, "document, document, document".
 So this is it, ladies and gentlemen, you can either put this book down right now and stop reading or move on and start the change that you want to see happening in your life!

 Your decision now is to change or not to change...
 So let's get on with it.

The Start of Something Great

 What I can be certain of is this. I wasn't the only one growing up with thoughts of being great, most, if not all kids, have a sense of great things, a positive outlook and ambition for their future; like becoming a spaceman, a pop singer or an explorer, but then something happens...

- Society -

 As we all know by now, especially after what happened with the 2016 US presidential election and the Uk leaving the EU (Brexit), associating yourself with like-minded people makes you more inclined to vote the same way as them. This is also what happens in your own life.

The majority of people find themselves in the same circle following the same path, never reaching their full potential.

Let me explain to you what I mean about society being the problem. As we are growing up, we are all taught to be workers and never leaders.

We have to learn to be leaders ourselves.

When children are taught in school, most are made to sing off the same hymn sheet. Learn and repeat, learn and repeat.

This is how the ultra, old-school rich can have anything and everything they want.

You and I are brought up to be "slaves" to study and then work within the system.

When we are growing up, we are educated in a certain way, then we work a job, perhaps more than one, but we work.

The majority are not aware of this system and live to work, survive and just pay the bills. It should, however, be the other way around and we should work towards something better and be fulfilling while realising our real goals and passions in life.

Most people in this situation would complain about the super-rich, "they aren't giving enough" or are jealous of them saying "I wish I could live a life like them and be as rich".

Forever jealous; always wanting what others have but never taking action. Always envious of others, comparing their lives when in reality they are not even doing a fraction of that the person they aspire to be has done.

I personally think that starting life at the bottom has its advantages because you'll never take anything for granted and you'll always have that fire in your belly to keep pushing yourself to the next level, in turn becoming enlightened and giving back to where you came from, "the bottom". A fantastic example of this is Richard Branson.

Do you think you are one of these people? Stuck in a job that you hate, feeling uninspired by what is around you, just going through the motions day in day out? Every day you are day dreaming about your next holiday, your next day off when you will finally win the lottery?

You work with people in the same exact situation, who think the same way, don't have the drive or motivation to think differently and are happy to follow the crowd. Those people around you who judge those who try to think outside the box. Are you stuck in this system?

I was one of these people too until I woke up and started paying attention.

You want what the people with everything have, "Success, wealth and freedom". You want it all.

The fact that you've bought this book and are now reading it shows that you want to make a change in your life. You have woken up from a very deep sleep when everyone else is still hibernating!

Congratulations!

Have a look around you, look at your friends, family and work colleagues. They are still asleep, working from week to week and never thinking that they can change their lives.
You know and feel it in your heart & soul that you can make that change.
Now is your time.
And in today's world, the world of the Internet, you can do it.
You can join the club of greatness and success.
And the best thing about it is that it won't take as long as it took them, you just need an idea and most important, the urge.

The Urge

I'm going to talk about the "Urge" before I get into talking about the "idea".
The "Urge" is something you want to have before you start building a business and a brand.
Without having the urge, you will fail.

If you started a business without the feeling of wanting to reach your ultimate goal, you might not succeed at all. If you found the urge then you are one of a kind, the lucky one and all of us should rub off you to see if we could catch the luck.
When you don't have the urge, you might give up when you fail once.
But if you have the urge and the want to succeed and keep pushing yourself forward, it won't matter how many times you fail. You'll continue to have that deep down feeling that will result in you achieving your goals to get where you wanna go in life.

I had the urge. Even though I've failed multiple times I always kept my head up.
It's like a funnel. We start at the edge and go round and round until we eventually make it through. With every failure, we learn new things about ourselves and about the process of making money.

I follow some successful influencers online, who have the urge to keep pushing themselves forward even after numerous failures until they finally had success. I would highly advise you to do the same, follow people you look up as this will help you to visualise where exactly you want to be and what you can also achieve if you put in the work.

One of my favourite influencers is Pat Flynn of SmartPassiveIncome.com - Pat wasn't always as successful as he is now. He started off as an architect and never even thought about starting an online business. It wasn't until he lost his job when the global recession happened that he felt the urge to change his path. He had to do something to keep himself and his family from going under.

So, it was with determination to succeed and a clear vision that helped Pat to use his knowledge and create an ebook on how to pass an architectural exam. With the success of his ebook he went on to create the Smart Passive Income blog, where he teaches, by example how to start your business online.

Pat did what you want to do, he woke up from the daily grind of working life and using the urge within himself, he created a fantastic brand and global following.

Look at Sylvester Stallone, Actor of such movies like Rocky & Rambo - When Sylvester was a young man he wrote a script for a movie. He went around from studio to studio looking for the movie to be funded and put into production.
The only thing he wanted was for him to be the star of his movie.

The majority of Studios turned him away saying a straight out "No", or "We like the script but not you as the star". At this time Sylvester was just about living on the street with his dog. It got so bad that he had to sell his dog to survive as he couldn't afford to feed it anymore. All the while he spent his time looking for someone to finance his movie idea. Eventually he got his funding, got his movie made with him as the star and was able to buy his dog back! The movie was Rocky.

Sylvester was at rock bottom but he never gave up! He had an awesome determination and an urge to live his dream and kept going until he was successful. This shows what drive and motivation can do for you!

Another example is Mike Dillard of the 'Self Made Man Podcast & Marketing Expert' - Mike has grown his companies to over $50 Million in revenue. Mike was not always a rich man, nor was he successful. He tells the story of him working as a waiter at a restaurant, spending all his free time after work (and during) reading and learning about making money. He says that his mistake, like many of us, was that he was chasing the money when he should have been aiming to help others.
When he realised his error he put his head down and educated himself on marketing and copywriting. Within 6 months Mike was successful.

Mike was trying to be rich by pursuing the money. He tried loads of different things to find that easy buck. But to be truely successful he turned his attention to helping people. And how did he achieve this? By educating himself first so that he could teach others.

What is apparent from these examples of three very successful people is that there is a recurring factor- They all had some failure before they had success!

Failure = *Success.*

Simple but true.

Most successful people have gone through a lot of failures to get where they are, without it they would have never taught themselves about what worked and what didn't.

That is one of the reasons I wrote this book. I've had failures, some big, some small, losing thousands of dollars in the process and wanted to share with you how can succeed and not fail and lose money on your journey like I or the three influencers did when we started out. I don't want you to give up after the first try or the first failure, I don't want you to walk away from what could be the defining moment of your life.
You have it in you to go after what you really want in life and not have regrets about what could have been! This is the start of your journey.

The book is structured into different parts to best help you climb the ladder of success.

The Idea Of Ideas

An idea can come from deep down or it can come to you in an instant!

I know, from personal experience, that without a concrete idea and focus you'll be running around in circles. You won't have any direction, just trying a variety of things at once without any structure or goal to aim for. Trust me, it will be a complete mess.

I, myself, spent three years like this. I did a bit of this and a bit of that but never fully focused on learning one thing or following through on one idea.

I learnt to build a website with WordPress, learnt about domain names, learnt about creating an App but never became a real master of anything. If I had focused on one idea I could have become an expert in that field. It's important to focus on an idea rather than trying to learn and do too much at one time.

If you want to be rich, (which most of us do) you'll have to commit. Get your head around learning and mastering one subject.

Become the master so you can teach the masses. That is the secret sauce, put in the hard work to become the master of your chosen profession.

If you are asking the question, "What can I master? I don't know anything about online and don't know what to do!" Don't fret, that's what I'm going to help you with throughout this book.

I also recommend that you learn about Copywriting. Over the years I've realised that to make a sale, you must have a good sales pitch. Good copy is extremely important if you want to sell and you will sell just about anything using it.

So decide what you want to learn and focus on and learn how to copyright.

I first heard this advice from one of my influencers Mike Dillard. I knew he was right.

Taking a step back and noticing what my influencers did was a big wake up point for me. The following people have gained success and influence by first having an idea and chasing after it with intense passion.

Pat Flynn acquired the skill of an affiliate. He now shares his monthly earnings on his website smartpassiveincome.com where he earns millions every year. He's an excellent example of where having an idea and a focus can lead you. I've come to trust in what he says and does. He is now a master of many things like podcasting and writing 'How to guides' but starting off he first focused on one.

Gary Vaynerchuk (Gary Vee), a social media genius, has gained a massive following online. Gary learned years ago from first making YouTube videos promoting his family business that social media is a great way for people to listen and become aware of you. He now has his own media company VaynerMedia.

Tony Robbins, a man who in my view, has mastered the skill of speech. People hang on to every word he says. He holds three-day seminars where he charges anything from $1,000 - $5,000 just to hear him talk with the promise of changing your life.

Mike Dillard, a global copywriting and marketing expert, who has amassed a fortune of $50 million+ by selling his books and courses. He has taught over a 1,000,000 people how to market online.

But right now you haven't mastered anything. I'm going to show you now how you can figure out what to master and where to go next, teaching you step by step, so you can be the next global influencer that others look up to and aim to be as successful as.

Are you ready to start taking action and get started on the rest of your life?!

I certainly hope so because you are responsible for your success and fulfilling your dreams.

This is not a get rich quick fast scheme. You will have to put in the work. I can show you the direction but cannot hold your hand and drag you along. I will provide you with the information you need to get there but you must take action and put in place what you learn.

Are you ready?...

Idea time

Coming up with an idea can be hard.

But if you follow the instructions that I'm going to give you right now it can actually be quite simple.

Depending on the environment that suits you, you could set up a quiet area or sit in a noisy coffee shop. Think about a place where you can think clearly, where you feel most inspired or creative.

Usually, great ideas come from great problems or great stresses.

The simplest ideas are usually the best; they create less work and less thought. The majority of ideas have been tried already and are out there in the World so it would be hard to come up with a new one. What I recommend you do is copy someone who is already doing what you want to do but in your own way. Put your own personal twist on it. Copy but don't copy!

There are thousands of marketers on Facebook, Google and in other places online, who are all trying to sell you something. Whether this is a course on how to do Facebook Ads or how to get thousands of email subscribers within a few days, you will see it all.

You might be thinking, "But I can't do the same as them"!

Well, I'm telling you that you can.

There are 7.6 billion people in the world (December 2017) and there is actually only a tiny proportion of people doing this kind of stuff online. So selling something like the next person who is already doing it is not a problem because you can target millions of people that won't ever see their Ad. The global market is yours for the taking.

Now, in your chosen environment, take out a notebook and using a pencil draw a circle in the middle of your page and write "IDEA" in the circle.

I want you to set a timer on a stopwatch or your phone. Set it for 2 mins. When you've done this I want you think hard about what hobbies you may have, the things you like to do, skills you have and what you'd like to learn about and using these examples branch out of your circle.

This is a mindmap to help you come up with your idea and focus so only write down the things you are really passionate about and want to be the master of. This could be what you are going to become known for and spend every waking minute thinking about and working towards so be selective. If you're not passionate now then you'll have to spend another 6-12 months learning something new!

The reason behind the timer is that if you've too much, it will be harder for you to decide what to do but if you have finished before the clock no worries, it makes it easier. Once you have done the first part of your mind map you will need to break those ideas you came up with into smaller segments.

Breaking them down into what you know about each until you have a clear path on which one you would like to become the master of.

When you find something that you would be passionate about doing then I recommend that you take that subject and learn everything there is to know about it. Be careful here with your choice, I've heard stories about people that have spent months learning certain skills that have then become outdated within a year or two so they had to start all over again. Choose something that will be around for years to come.

Read the books, study the courses, listen to the podcasts. Eventually, you will be so knowledgeable about that subject you'll be able to sing it.

If you see any interesting information about your skill online save it. This could be useful for future reference. Remember, everything you want to learn is available online for FREE. It's just up to you to get started. The information is there, it's written in Blogs, on YouTube, in Facebook groups, through free Courses and on Podcasts.

If there is one thing you take away from this first chapter it is to :

"Educate", Learn and Implement".

Brand Up Bitch

Creating a personal brand or company brand is one of the most important factors in becoming successful. You want people to identify with your brand and be aware of who you are/ or what your business stands for the minute they see your name or logo. Recognisable branding is what all successful businesses strive for.

Can you name five brand names off the top of your head that started out doing one thing but are now able to sell many different things to a number of different markets due to having become a recognisable and trusted brand?

Examples of such brands and entrepreneurs are:

- Apple
- McDonald's
- Google
- Microsoft
- Virgin
- Coca-Cola company
- Tim Ferris

- Tyra Banks

- Kim Kardashian

- Gary Vaynerchuk

- Oprah Winfrey

These successful entrepreneurs and companies have set their businesses up in such a way that people don't just buy for the product they create or advertise, they buy for the brand name and brand identity because of the trust they have in that person and business.

That is what you, as an up and coming entrepreneur should focus on, the brand of you.

You won't just hear this from me, it is repeated over and over by other successful entrepreneurs.

To get started with the "brand of you", I recommend going first to a domain registrar. The one I choose over others is GoDaddy.com. This is where I pick up all my domain names.

You're going to buy the most important domain name you'll ever buy, your name!

Only thing is though unless you've thousands of dollars, you're not going to pick up your first name. Like mine "Daniel.com" is not available and if I wanted to pick that up, it would cost 5 to 6 figures. So search for your full name, first & last.

I would recommend you to get the .com if you can because dot com is the most trustworthy domain name available, it's a tld (top-level-domain) and that is King.

If your full name is available in .net or .org that's ok too. They are like being the Queen & Joker.

The same goes for a brand name; if you intend on going down that route with your business. Be sure to get the dot-com version of your name because if your company or business is successful in the future you won't want to have to pay millions just to have the .com version of your name.

If you can't acquire the .com, go for .net or .org and you'll be fine.

If you have not yet thought about what you'd call your business but know what industry it's in or have a keyword for it like "Business" or "Launch" etc. You can find a few options to help you find the best brand name by using the following sites.

- LeanDomainSearch.com

- ExpiredDomains.net

First, go to LeanDomainSearch.com. Here you will find a search bar with a bunch of popular keywords underneath. Type in the keyword that you think that would suit your business and click search.

You will then see examples of names that could be a potential business name for your brand.

If you click to buy, you'll be brought to GoDaddy.com to purchase the domain name.

Secondly, you could go to ExpiredDomains.net. This website is great for picking up names that have some history behind them. These names were either bought before and dropped or are now in auction.

Go to the menu and look for "Domain Lists" then click on the first item that shows "GoDaddy Closeouts". These are domains that were recently dropped and you can pick them up for less than $25, some with traffic and age.

Use the filter here by clicking "show filter".

Type in the keyword you want in your business name, you can choose if you want it at the start, middle or end of your domain name.

On this same filter menu, you will see a tab saying "TLDs", tick the dot-com & dot net. There are other filters here and even more, if you sign up, like how many names you want to see on one page, is the Facebook or Twitter handle has been taken and names with or without numbers.

Apply the filter.

Now the list that was showing with useless words has now shortened to a few pages. Search to see if there is a suitable name for your business, if not use the tactics I explained and try again.

You could also search to see if there is a name in auction or for sale, however with this option, you could end up paying a few hundred to a few thousand for a half decent name.

Once you find your name or buy your own the next step will be to set it up.

There are a variety of ways to set up your domain name. You can set up hosting, forward it to a destination or use a third party to connect it with. Do your due diligence and decide what type of website you want to create.

For your brand, I would recommend using landing page software to create your homepage so that you'll be able to get viewers to convert to customers.

Front End

There are two important things you need to grab people's attention...

The first is to give them something of interest, something they want ...and the second is your Front End, this is the page where you will need to convert visitors into customers.

Without these two vital things nothing else will fit together properly and you'll have no hope of achieving success.

Let's say that I have a product, but no front end, what would ultimately happen?

I would not be able to convert people into email subscribers.

Now let's say that I have a front end but no real product?

I would not be able to convert them because I wouldn't have anything of value to give them.

That, however, might not be the case in all situations.

People often subscribe and hand over their emails without getting value right away, instead, they receive it over the long run with the provider still having to give them value later down the line.

I find that these two things, product and front end, can not only make you successful but can make you a lot of money.

Collecting email subscribers is the gold at the end of the rainbow. It's what all online marketers strive to achieve. To grow their subscriber base to hundreds of thousands and eventually millions as many entrepreneurs have shown possible.

Why do they strive to achieve this?

Because with this....

You don't have to target people with ads to sell something

You don't have to introduce yourself or your business every time to make a sale

You can make 100% profit from selling to your subscribers (email list)

You don't even have to make your own products. You can up sell affiliate products that you've used and would recommend.

Repeat customer spend

I could go on and on.

But that is the ultimate goal that we hope to achieve over the course of this book.

To grow your subscribers by...

Coming up with an idea

Developing your own personal Brand

Creating a free guide or giving away a free gift

Building a community of like-minded people that will buy anything from you

Using the tools to collect, interact and make money from your subscribers

Creating Copy to grab the attention of your potential followers

Advertise for free and make money for life

The steps that I have written above are my Steps to Success.

It might seem a little overwhelming and look like a lot to do but it's really not.

As mentioned earlier, you need to focus on one thing first and become an 'expert' in this chosen field.

These are steps that I myself have followed and succeeded with. I'm giving you this book for free in the hope too that you will follow the same steps and have your own success.

To receive this book you gave me your email. Then I offered to teach you everything I know in detail throughout the book.

I show you how to do this, step by step, using my training and personal insight into to help you to achieve your goals and have financial freedom in the long term.

In one of my funnels I share my one time offer, which is a 15min phone call with me. Then I provide an upsell in which I offers a one-hour Mentoring and last of all a one time only offer of Mentoring for two months in a private Facebook Community in which I will make sure you that you succeed.

The reason that collecting email subscribers is so important, is that once you have someone signed up to your mailing list, you are able to reach out to them and send them an email offering your services and products whenever you have something to offer, that could potentially benefit their lives and be of great value to them. In this way, you will not have to spend any extra money on acquiring new subscribers. By doing this you can gain 100% profit. And, unless they unsubscribe, you will have the possibility of having them as repeat customers indefinitely.

Offering your advice on tools, books, courses, using affiliate links etc can make you hundreds and thousands every time you send out an email to your list.

Leaving you to live the life that you've always dreamed of and even make money while you sleep.

And that's only part of it, the best part is being able to give back and help others who were in your same situation improve their lives and get out of the 'follow the crowd' mindset.

Helping others, that can't help themselves or are held back because of difficult circumstances.

That is what it's all about. It's possible for everyone to have success if hard work is put in from the beginning.

If you have success and knowledge then I feel that it's important to help others when you are equipped with the necessary means. But, right now, you must help yourself so you can do all this in the future.

Put the money you make into your education now, whether that is online or through mentors and teachers, learn from the best, people like Pat Flynn, Gary Vaynerchuk, Ramit Sethi and Mike Dillard. These are much more are giving their time and knowledge to help people like you so that you can eventually make a difference in the world. All of you are blessed with your own talent and gift and have something to offer so find out what this is and go for it without reservation.

Many of the worlds most influential people give their knowledgeable for free but will also charge you, so that you will invest in yourself. It's proven that if you pay for something you will make more of an effort than if you were to get that same information or product for free.

These people want you to put in the work and not waste any of their precious time.

I've downloaded free ebooks and reports hundreds of times, but for most, I never put the effort in and read them. However, the materials I've bought, I've treasured, respected and consumed as if they were going to be taken away from me any moment.

Are you now ready to get stuck into the front end and what it should look like, how it works and how to get people to hand you over their email address to you?

Front End Page

Like I've said, the front end is no good without being able to collect emails. I'll show you in the next chapter how to sign up to an email subscriber account on MailChimp, build your 5-day emails and the content you should include to catch a persons attention and get them to input that all important email.

But for now, the front end page.

Have you ever booked a hotel or accommodation from an online travel provider, like Booking.com or Airbnb.com?

Have you spent hours looking for the right place to stay, checking each page for the description, images, reviews, videos, location and what they can provide you with?

I take it that most of you have.

When you visit these websites you will have a look at the top reviewed or the top booked places in your chosen destination. I bet that most people that booked a trip booked it online rather than offline.

To get people to book with them over others these bookings pages would have to everything possible to enable them to convert well. They have thought of everything.

The images are to die for

The location is perfect

The facilities are amazing

And the reviews are outstanding.

These are all the things that you should consider for your own front page. These sites have been doing this for years and know what works and doesn't.

You should include the following:

Eye-catching, inspiring or motivating images or video to create a want or desire in your subscriber

Description of what you or your business is all about.

What exactly it is that you are selling

What value you can provide them with

Include reviews (Hint *if you have no review yet then do a giveaway to a few people and ask for a review)

There is also another way to do this, for you to see exactly what type of page converts well.

You can basically copy the same format as the page you like, that's already working and start converting people right away.

Firstly you'll have to know what business you're getting into and then search for the top 10 people in that particular business.

As an example for this book, I'll stick with marketing businesses. I'll explain how to find out what pages they're using to convert visitors and how to copy them.

You might have a totally different business to marketing but it doesn't matter, there is money to be made in any business, you'll just have to figure out what your customers want.

Tip * I recommend checking out the book "Ask" by Ryan Levesque, a proven online formula to discover exactly what your customers want to buy.

You can search for the top 10 influencers in your chosen market on SimilarWeb.com and see what ads or landing pages they use to drive their business. Using this will enable you to see all the data you'll need to create your own front page. I DON'T, however, recommend or condone copying these influencers word for word as you could be brought to court for copy infringement and you are not being honest or genuine with your own customers.

On the website overview, you'll be able to see where traffic is coming from. This includes countries people are searching from to what top referring websites and social sites are leading back to the influencers own website.

You'll be able to see the top 10 common traits that they use, whether it's pictures, videos or something totally different. You don't have to do anything from scratch in this day and age as these landing pages have all been tried and tested so find one that works for you and try it out making some changes to suit your brand and product.

If you can't find out what ads or landing pages your competitors or top influencers use then I would advise to go directly to their website and look at how they entice you to sign up. What steps do they take to lead you to sign up to their mailing list? Take in all aspects of their page as there may be something very small but persuasive that you can also use.

Usually, when you visit websites they will re-target you on social networks using cookies to get you to sign up so that you can become part of their subscriber base. Cookies are another fantastic way to retarget customers once they have left your site. Using these you are reminding them that you are still there and they can always come back.

See how they do it and create similar front pages to capture emails.

The Tools You Can Use To Build One

When building a front or landing page, as they are called, there are a number of routes you can take.

I will talk about two of these because I know that these websites will still be relevant in 5-10 years.

They are also very easy to use.

One is free and the other has a trial option so you can decide if it is for you. They are both brilliant for capturing emails and I recommend trying out both to see which is best and most relevant for your business.

You will need to use an email provider like MailChimp, which I will explain about further in the next chapter.

The tools that I personally used and would highly recommend are:

• Wordpress

• ClickFunnels

WORDPRESS

First, let's talk about Wordpress. Building a landing page on Wordpress is actually not that hard.

There are thousands of different plugins that you can use to build a great looking Website and hundreds of free themes that you can use to help you to stand out from the crowd. You also have the choice of purchasing a premium theme to suit the website you are building.

I use Wordpress for my primary website DanielMacSweeney.com and a few others.

Anyway, enough of promoting how good Wordpress is, we'll move onto the "How to create a landing page that works".

Let's imagine that you don't have a website yet. You have your idea and now you want a page where people can go to find out what you are all about and give you their email.

The first thing you should do is have everything for your landing page written down.

This is the information that will tell visitors what you or your company are all about.

Use bullet points and the information that I've spoken about previously.

Like how the hotel or travel sites do it...

Use:

Eye-catching, inspiring or motivating images or video to create a want or desire in your subscriber

Description of what you or you business is all about.

What exactly it is that you are selling

What value you can provide them with

Include reviews

Get stuck into that before you move onto anything else.

If you have created your Wordpress website with your domain name then sign in.

Search for the theme that you think would suit your business and install it. I would find a theme where you'll be able to change the structure, one that has building blocks so you can change the way your front page looks.

After you have done this, go to your plugins and install the recommended ones suggested by Wordpress along with a Wordpress plugin.

Once you've done that it's time to create your landing page.

Come up with something similar to one of your influencers landing pages. It's good to copy but not copy in an identical way. Take ideas from their site. That way, you'll know that it's a good page for converting if that's what they are using themselves.

Put in all the front page information that you've written down and you will then have set up your very first landing page.

Congratulations.

The next step is to head over to MailChimp and sign up for an account. Follow the instructions on how to integrate your account with Wordpress and Insert an email form on your landing page for collecting emails.

You will need to build more pages on Wordpress if you want to bring people through your funnel to up sell on your products or courses.

It's not a difficult thing to do but there is a bit of work to all this.

This is something I teach my students in my Mentoring Masterclass at DanielMacSweeney.com/Mentor.

The only thing it will cost you other than hosting and a domain name is your time and energy.

CLICKFUNNELS

This is one of the handiest tools on the internet. You don't even need hosting, just an email provider like MailChimp and a Domain name to get started.

Created by Russell Brunson, of "DotCom Secrets" Russell's been creating funnels for years.

He created this website so that you can build a landing page within minutes instead of hours.

There is a 14-day trial, if you sign up after the trial period it will cost $100 dollars a month.

Click funnels does more than creating one landing page for you. You can bring customers through a series of funnels creating more of a chance to make money and convert a fan for life, which is exactly what you want as these fans will always buy your stuff over and over again.

There are loads of different types of funnels that you can use and all can be set up pretty fast.

When you sign up to Click Funnels, you'll be brought through a step by step on how to create the perfect funnel for your business.

So, there is no need for me to get into it here.

In the next chapter I'm going to talk all about :

MailChimp

The 5 most important emails you'll need to convert subscribers to buyers, and converting these buyers into lifetime fans.

Email And The x 5 Hello's

In the last chapter, we spoke about the importance of a landing page.

People in the off-line world build businesses every day. It can often take them years to make a real profit. Start-up costs can be anywhere from low to high thousands.

Off-line businesses usually make their money from selling physical products, their time or information and rarely make money while they sleep.

They put in a huge amount of work, working all the hours that God gave them and can sometimes struggle to keep themselves afloat.

Paying rent, rates, taxes, employee costs etc... it all adds up. There is a lot more cost in the 'Bricks and Morter' set up than doing business online.

These offline businesses can only target customers when the customer is somewhere specific, for example using a shop window display or poster/advert and would have to showcase their product or themselves to a group in a location where there is only a limited number of people to sell to rather than millions/billions.

You must also take into account the travel costs, accommodation, staff, food etc... and these costs can amount to thousands every year.

The steps to starting a business online can be similar to offline but it is much easier online as the customer is available immediately. The majority of people are 'online' these days and have internet access, with the smartphone being the number tool in accessing and targeting your online market.

There are some major differences between Online and Offline:

Little or no work once you have it set up and running (Tim Ferris calls this the 'Four hour work week').

Work remotely- Meaning you can work from anywhere in the World, beside the pool in your Villa, from the beach, in an exciting city that will inspire you daily etc.

Make money while you sleep.

You'll never have to go to sleep again, worrying about getting up in the morning and having to travel to work, just to earn a living if you put in the work now to build your online presence.

There are:

Little or no initial start up costs.

It has become so much easier to make money with a huge increase in online shopping and learning happening online. People are looking for ease of access and you can give them that by targeting them directly online.

More free-time to live life now and not wait until you are retired.

The last point is my favourite part of making money online. It has enabled me to spend my extra time doing what's most important to me, spending it with family and friends, without being exhausted from the daily grind.

Sell too many and not a few

The greatest thing about online business is that instead of being limited to a few hundred people in one area you can sell to millions, Worldwide!

These are a few points about making money online and is a factor in why you need an email list of cheering fans right away. Build your brand and sell whatever you want.

All you need do to have everything I've just mentioned, to make money while travelling, never have to go to work to make money again with no freedom when instead you can make it from your house, on the train, by the beach, with little or no costs, ultimately give you time with your loved ones -

....is to grow an email list.

Why?

Because, once you have all this setup and have built up trust with your subscribers, all you have to do is send an email to your list offering or selling them something that they "Want, not just need", and you can make hundreds or thousands every week.

Mike Dillard, one of my Mentors, tells an antidotal about himself about when he sent just three emails to his subscribers.

He didn't have to make or create anything. All he did was talk about how great an already existing product was, which in this case was an affiliate link to join a yearly newsletter on the stock market, making him over $250,000 in a few days. All because people trusted Mike's advice.

That's the type of growth potential I'm talking about, what we are aiming for with this book.

Setting up Mailchimp

When I first discovered Mailchimp I found it slightly confusing but after playing around with different options it got real easy.

After you sign up to Mailchimp you'll need to create a list. This is where all your collected emails go when people sign up on your front end page.

One of the great aspects of MailChimp is that it allows you to use auto responders right away so that you can send daily emails to new subscribers, and in doing so, you'll be able to grow your dedicated fan base.

When you create a list you'll be able to show your Subscriber who the email is from.

Make sure you make this clear as day, because, sometimes when a person signs up to an email list, they forget who you are and why they signed up in the first place.

Become the charismatic character as Russel Brunson has called it in his book 'Dot.com secrets'.

Where you tell the receiver your backstory, your journey, where you want to go and what you want to achieve and how you can help them during this.

The first few emails that they receive are the most important you'll ever send. It is, with these, that you must catch their intention and reel them in.

Make sure your name is clear and the reason why they signed up to you in the first place is there.

Next, you'll have to build sign up forms. These are the links where people give you their details and join your list. You can create your own or follow the templates provided by MailChimp which are what I would personally recommend.

I use general forms to make my emails and use the link in them to get people to sign up.

You can use these on your website to send someone to sign up. These links can also be integrated into Facebook, Twitter, Instagram and many more places online.

In your 'Sign up form' let the new subscriber know:

Why they are subscribing and what the benefit to them will be.

You can use the MailChimp template or edit it to create your own, adding pictures or videos.

Once they sign up, they will first get an Opt-in confirmation email.

You'll then need to send them a response message once they have clicked the link in the opt-in...

You can send them a Thank you message with any information you that you want to share with them.

First and foremost you will want to welcome them, talk to them as if you are face to face, let them know what you'll be sharing, why they are important to you, how you can help them and also give them a gift.

Gifts are important, as it's probably the reason they signed up in the first place, and if not, they will respect you more for giving them something of value in return.

Hint- Let them know that your gift is valuable and that it's only for a select few. This will make you more rememberable, which is important if you want to make sales from them in the future.

If you want to learn all about setting up your email responder, I can mentor you on this step by step. Just head over to my website DanielmacSweeney.com and send me a message.

This can make it easier for you if you want the Exact Formula I and the experts use. [LINK]

The Five Hellos

We are now going to dive deep into the 'Five Hellos'. The five emails that your brand new subscribers will receive within the first few days after subscribing to your email list.

These emails are some of the most important emails you'll ever send, because, with these emails, you'll start moulding and creating a dedicated fanbase. A fan who will buy anything from you and will spread the word on who you are to their closest friends and family.

The best form of advertising is Word of Mouth which is used by huge brands and businesses globally, such as clothing retailer Ted Baker. For Ted Baker it is all about the experience, the follow-up service and making their customer feel special, ensuring that these customers spread the word about the brand rather than them having to spend huge money on advertising. If you follow the steps I'm going to show you below, you also won't have to spend money on ads. People will come to you...

These five emails are not spoken about as much as they should be by the online professionals and mentors.

Russell Brunson is one of the few I've heard talk about them in detail in his book "DotCom Secrets". He also mentions that he is not the creator of this formula, that it was created by Andre Chaperon and is used by most of the experts online.

He calls it the Soap Opera Sequence.

Once I saw this formula, I had an "Aha" moment.

The sequence can be as long as you want it to be, however, Russell recommends five emails and I also believe this is the right amount.

Why?

Because, people in today's society are constantly rushing, everything is on fast forward and information needs to be instantaneous.

If you really want to get someone's attention, follow the KISS method.

K eep

I t

S imple

S illy

You don't want to bombard and bore people with emails every day for 6 months and you don't want them to forget who you are either, so five messages are enough for them to get interested in you and remind them that you are there.

If you feel that you need more, that's fine, don't worry about it too much. Just remember that people want quick fixes and don't want do things long term cos "People are Lazy!" Unfortunately, this is a very true statement. The majority of people want an immediate fix that doesn't call for too much work or action to be taken by them. Try to provide them with the best information in the shortest, most informative way possible.

This is how you should structure your 'Five Hellos'.

First of all, it's a good idea to have something to sell them in the fourth and fifth email, this will be important for growing your subscriber list for free.

I will go through the reason for this in an upcoming chapter.

It doesn't have to be your own product. Just something you recommend and have used that you think would also be great for them.

Think about what Mike Dillard did to make over $250,000 in a space of a week, he used an affiliate product.

You can find affiliates on loads of different websites such as:

Amazon Affiliate's

Cj.com

JVZoo.com

ClickFunnels.com

Some companies and business don't have their affiliate products listed on these websites so you should also check their own websites for the best affiliate product that suits your branding.

I'd ultimately stick to one of the above listed as they are the easiest and fastest to use. And if anything goes wrong with the product you have a middleman to step in and dispute the issue.

What do you write about in these "*Five Hellos*"?

What should you say?

How can you get people to click on and buy from your affiliate link or your product?

Follow these steps:

Set the stage – Tell a story about you or someone else that the reader can relate to.

High Drama, Backstory and the Wall – Make it exciting, get into detail about the backstory and explain the hardship that happened to you.

- **Epiphany & The One Thing –**

This is the amazing thing you found that helped you succeed on your journey.

- **Hidden Benefits –**

Explain why it helped you and why only it could.

- **Urgency –**

Set a time limit or set only a certain amount left before the thing is gone. This will give them little time to decide and get them purchasing your item as soon as possible.

Once these five Very Important steps are followed you should have an everlasting fan who'll buy everything from you and have also have made a sale in the fourth or fifth sequence email.

The priority here was getting them to first sign up to you, the next is to continue holding onto them as a subscriber so if you didn't make a sale during your 5 email sequence do not worry.

You can message them as much or as little as you want from now on unless they unsubscribe.

I would suggest once or twice a week, this is plenty if you don't want to scare them off.

It's a known fact that it usually takes 8 follow-ups for someone to buy from you and with your Five Hellos, you'll already be on track to start making money.

As you have seen from the above, having your email set up from the start to enable you to get subscribers from the get-go is a must.

In the next chapter, I'm going to show you how to set up a Facebook page the right way...

Creating a Facebook Page

Setting up a Facebook page is not difficult in the slightest, however, there are many things that people miss starting out when setting up their Brand page on Facebook.

I'm going to show you exactly how to set one up the right way, step by step.

The first thing you'll need to do is head to the top of the Facebook page and on the blue bar on the right-hand side, you should see a small dark arrow pointing down. Click that and you'll see a drop-down menu.

On the menu, you'll see the words "Create Page". Click on that to get started on building your Facebook Page.

When you come to the next page, you'll have six options to choose from. Choose the one that is relative to the niche you're in and also decide if you are going to sell Products or Content or be a Brand or an influencer.

If you've made the right selections then choosing the category your business fits into here will be very simple.

As an example, I would select 'Brand or Product'. Then I would select 'Brand' from the list of categories. Then I would need to enter the name of my business. eg. "TheBrandAgency".

Remember, the name all depends on you and the business you're getting into, so have your name chosen with all this in mind and enter it here. Another thing you must be

For now, edit the username and change it to the name of your business, if your name is taken, you could always put "The" in front of your brand name or use numbers.

This is important for advertising purposes so that you can send people to the right place to check out your business by telling them to go to HTTPS: //Facebook .com/your brand name.

Next, write a description for your page, take your time doing this, write down some good Copy which is understandable and clear. Describe what your business does, what you hope to achieve and how you can help.

If your business uses calls and organises meetings with clients then include your phone number and address for this purpose. You can leave this blank for the time being until you've organised everything else.

If you can't describe what your business does in one sentence, get out of that business. If it's too complicated for you, it's too complicated for your customers.

Back on your homepage, go to 'Add a button'. This is a button you can use to send visitors to a targeted destination. It's always good to use the link you used in your post.

You can even see the insights into how many people are clicking on it each week by hovering over the button itself and clicking "View Insights".

Next, go to settings to leave a "messenger greeting", for anyone trying to contact you so that you can also use this as a targeted area to send people to the right places. Scroll down on the left-hand side and go to 'Messaging'. At 'Show a Messenger Greeting' click yes.

Click on the text to editing the replying message. Welcome them and send them to your link.

I also want to show you how your page can be found on Facebook. There are other ways, but to start off with before you do anything else, head to "Edit your Details". Add in three words that describe your business where categories are. These are link hashtags and, when typed into Facebook, your page will be part of that particular category.

Here you should also enter your website so when people do check out your 'About' details they can go directly to that destination.

Last but not least, add your page to shortcuts.

To do this, click on the button with the three dots on your page. Four up from the bottom of the list you'll see 'Pin to Shortcuts', when you do this it will be added to your Facebook homepage sidebar so you can get to your page a lot faster than looking for it each time.

Set Up A Facebook Group

Now that you know how to set up a Facebook Page I want to show you how to set up a Facebook Group.

As I've said before, focus on one at a time, either grow your page or grow your group, especially when you're starting out.

But it doesn't hurt to set up the other one now anyway so that when you do come to grow the other one you can just jump right in.

I didn't start building my Facebook Page until I knew my Group was on an upward trend and had my dedicated fans.

So...

Let's get started on building a Facebook Group!

It's just as easy to set up a group as it was a page. Go to the top blue bar on Facebook where you'll see a dark grey arrow pointing down. Click on that and you'll see the words 'Create Group'.

Once you've clicked on "Create Group" you'll get a pop up where you will have to give your group a name.

For demonstration purposes, I'm going to call it "TEST".

To start a group, you'll need to have at least one other person join it, so you'll have to invite someone. When you're starting out you don't have to invite everyone, just invite a friend or a loved one to get the ball rolling. Let them know what you are doing and what you want to achieve. (This is good practice for you to be able to talk about your business and describe it to others.

At the bottom of this pop up, you'll see a little box that says "Pin to Shortcuts". Tick that so you can get back to your group faster from your profile page in the future.

Then click Create.

Now that you've created a group another pop up should show. The header for this pop up will have your new brand name.

Choose an icon that represents your business. If you are a musician click that or if you are a sports team, a community, etc use that.

Once you hit Okay you'll be brought to the actual group page. It will need a banner, a description and tags similar to your Facebook page.

Start with the image that you had created on either Fiverr, 99Designs, 20DollorBanners or WordSwag.

Click on the green button to upload the image.

In the description, you can use something similar to your Facebook page or choose to write a completely new one.

Trust me when I say, the description is going to change a few times before you feel like it's perfect.

After you've given your group a description, you'll also need to add tags. So that your group can be found by other people.

To do this click on the three dots on the group menu bar. A drop-down menu will show, click on 'Edit Group Settings' to change and add what your group is about.

Here you can choose what group type you want to show people you are.

Edit the description.

And enter tags so your group can be found in the Facebook search engine.

Choose tags that suit what your business is all about, these are the keywords which people would type into the Facebook search engine.

Another great way to get followers and be found organically is to provide a location. 'Edit Location' to type in where your business is located and the local community will now be able to see your brand as a suggested page and when people search that area your business might show up in the results providing you with more likes and followers.

In the settings, you'll also be able to edit your Facebook web address and email. At the moment your web address is a bunch of numbers so when you click on 'Change Address' a popup shows.

Here you can edit your Facebook Web Address to your business name like "Facebook .com/groups/YourWebAddress and also your Facebook email address to YourBrandName@groups.facebook .com

Save these changes and your Facebook Group is almost ready to launch...

Fill Your Group With Content

Creating content can be one of the most time-consuming tasks that you'll have to deal with in your business.

Every day, you will have to provide value and content to your group to keep them engaged and active.

There are hard ways to doing this, messy ways, and ways that can create groups full of junk and spam.

I want to show you the easy way, the organised way to create an extremely valuable community.

The way that you can bring, amazing value to your members and create a dedicated fan base that will in the future purchase anything from you.

The steps I'm going talk about and show you are

Threads, Live, Likes and comment.

To begin with Threads.

Threads are a fantastic way to keep a group engaged and active.

First, you'll need to come up with what you want to share with your group and write them down.

The ones that I'd recommend are:

Blogs, creating a thread for people to share their blogs or blog posts is great, because having it in one place for people to read, makes it easier for members to see other peoples content and it stops the main feed is filled up with people trying to promote their blogs.

Promotion thread, my god every group should have this. At least 5% of my day is deleting posts that are promotions.

People trying to sell stuff, promote affiliate links and sharing, useless spammy content.

A promotion thread is a must have when you are running a group. It's only natural as internet marketers we want to share our products and make a bit of money online, and sharing them to groups and pages can be a free way to do it.

When groups allow this type of promotion on their main feed, eventually other people that were enjoying the content will move on, and the group will stagnate, because these people are not in the group to buy stuff, to begin with, they are there to learn and be entertained. That's why a promotion thread is very important, so your group doesn't get spammy.

Lessons is another way to get people engaged and to keep them sweet. By you sharing lessons (valuable content), people will come to like you and look up to you, and eventually, after they get to know you, by listening and watching you, you'll become their fearless leader.

There are other types of threads you can use to keep people engaged and active. Yours might be different to mine, but these are the examples that I use, other than the ones I've just mentioned.

Motivation

Fundays

Vlogs

Podcasts

Connect

Now, the way you can post threads can be up to you. You could go completely random and post on these threads whenever you want to bring them to the top of the feed.

You could re-pin threads on certain days, weeks or months.

It's up to you.

I find that going random, is a good thing because it makes it different every day.

When you have a list of threads created, post them into your Rules on the pinned tab and to make it easy for the members to get to these threads, use Hashtags.

What I mean is something like this #Promote, but if you use that hashtag, your thread could get lost very fast, because other people on Facebook could be using the same one.

So, you'll have to make you're hashtag unique like I have for Financial Freedom Forever, to send people to a certain thread. I use hashtag #PromoteFFF to make it a one of a kind hashtag. So when people click on that hashtag in my pinned rules tab or other hashtags I've created, they see nothing but my threads and posts.

To make these threads more unique and easy to find, create an image to post with a particular thread and even have the name of the thread written in the image.

This makes it look much better and also easier to find.

Going Live to you're audience, is the most Personal and most upfront way to communicate and get your message across. Facebook makes going live a priority as when you go Live, everyone that follows you will get a notification that you are.

This doesn't happen for posts, images or video.

So, going Live is also the fastest way to become influential, as people will begin to watch you and put you on a pedestal. You'll become a rock star in their eyes.

Going Live is still fairly new, so you might be a bit nervous at the start. There are groups you can join to get over the fear of going live.

I've set up a group, just for this if you want to shake off the fear.

It took me 4 to 5 goes before getting in front of my audience and as it gets bigger it's still nerve-racking but enjoyable.

People will get to know you this way and trust you. I find that people don't buy stuff for the sake of it online, they buy off someone or some brand they trust. Going Live is personal and that way you can create trust in a short space of time.

Liking and commenting.

These two tactics are ones that I find that keep people talking and engaged. I've even been asked on my Group why do I keep liking my own stuff.

I personally think that it makes the post look like it's active to people that see it, pulling them in to interact and like it also.

And when you like and comment on other people's posts, it provides them with positive feedback. This lights up parts of their brain area which processes reward feelings about things like food, sex, money, and social acceptance.

This type of interaction is a powerful one to mould you into an all-knowing, likeable influencer.

This is how to keep you're group active and alive.

Do these things and you'll have a dedicated fan base, who'll buy anything from you.

Fill Your Page With Content

Filling your page with content is a bit different than creating content in a group.

Here you are the only one posting and creating interaction with the people that are following you.

The questions you'll need to ask yourself first are:

What kind of business am I?

Depending on what you share, depends on what you do. Let's say you are in the tourist industry, and what you do is walking tours.

What do you post?

You post pictures and videos of the views where you walk, the people that you guide and the daily struggles and enjoyments of what you do.

Food you take and gear you use.

You are trying to engage your followers in a conversation. Even if you don't or can't create this content for some reason, it's there to share from YouTube, blog posts and news sites.

This is how many large Facebook pages grew.

If you were in the Hotel or B&B business, you post pictures and content of your accommodation and what you're area has to offer, the activities and the people that are involved in you're area etc

Like I said, depending on what business you are in, you're posts will be different.

But in general, if you use these types of posts I share with you, you'll create interaction and sales between you and your follower and your content will be shared, which in turn will grow your followers.

Quotes & Questions

If you use imagery with quotes & questions you'll have more of a chance of receiving engagement with your followers.

Use bright images, images that stand out and call for an action to happen.

When you do post something, I mean anything, it's a good idea to leave a comment in your post or get your partner to leave one.

This will show to people that see the image or post that it must be interesting, and they will click into it to see what's going on, as us humans are very inquisitive and don't want to be left behind.

Videos

Create your own or take from YouTube.

Nowadays creating your own video is simple, use your phone. You don't need some fancy high def camera to take good videos.

If you sell products video the products, show how they work, use them in real life. You don't need a video production team or the gear that goes with it.

If you use video from YouTube always compliment the creator of the video, hashtag them, that way you might get a comment or shared or followed by people that follow them or even referred by the creator.

Once your page gets big enough you could do give aways. This is a great way to get followers interacting with a post.

You could ask them to leave a comment to win something that you provide.

Sometimes by doing this, you can grow your sales by multiple because, if you think about it, if one person comments that has 100 friends, then one of their friends comments on it, that has a 1,000 friends the engagement can be massive. And all that matters is people's attention.

If you sell products through your page, show pictures of them, use links and descriptions in the posts. Facebook has lowered viewers who see your posts to slow down spam, how to overcome this is to post at least four or five times a day on your page. Stay active, the more people that see your posts, the more they will see it on their feed.

Organise Yourself

Now that we've built a page or community, we need to organise ourselves so that when people come to join us, we look professional and we look like we know what we're talking about.

To start off with go to your own Facebook profile, the one your friends and family see. Here we need to edit a few things.

First use a clear image of yourself for your profile picture, so that people can see your face and the upper part of your torso.

You want to create a sense of, reflective imagery. What I mean is, some people will judge you on how you look and how you posture yourself, they'll think without realising, "Is this person like me".

This will create Trust!

Next, background image. Here you can use a video or an image. Use something that reflects who you are, where you're from or what you do. Don't use silly or insulting images, and also create your own, don't copy other people's backgrounds as it looks very unprofessional and misleading.

This background area is a fantastic way to influence people and explain who you are, it's one of the first things people will see when they come to your profile.

Use it as a call to action, tell the people that see it, to sign up, or use a code to get 50% off or something like that. They'll tell their friends and there Friends will tell theirs, and you'll have hundreds of people watching your background video, just for that reason alone.

Edit your description, keep it short, straight to the point. People's attention spans are short nowadays, so introduce yourself, describe what you do and call to action, ask them to do something.

It's amazing how many people will do something when told.

After you finish editing your description there is an area on your profile where you can insert links (URLs).

This is another way to get people to use a call to action. When anyone comes to your profile, they will do one of the three things, look at your picture, look at your posts or click your link.

Before we get into growing a following, one of the most important things to present yourself well is to fill your profile with like-minded content.

Whatever niche or business you're in post content for a few days on your feed that has something to do with your niche. This can be Images, quotes, stories, or news posts from websites.

Edit your social networks for to grow your followers on other platforms.

Now, the last thing to do is start growing.

Go to the search bar on Facebook and type the keyword to do with your niche. Then go to groups and join around 20 to 50 groups and become a member.

Do the same with pages, like 20 to 50 again and get ready to take interest.

You are going to replicate what these groups and pages are doing but create something better for your audience. You'll see what's working and what's not. What people are commenting on and what they are interacting with.

Once you're accepted into the groups, post a thank you post and introduce yourself.

Remember, you're not selling anything or inviting anyone to business yet. Offer your help & advice. Do this for a few days, post daily in these groups and comment on the pages.

Believe it or not, people will contact you to find out what you're all about. Share some knowledge and show that you know what you're talking about in your industry. This way, you are creating an image for yourself that people can trust and remember.

I could list off a few people that are in groups that I am involved with and they are very active, and because they are, they have massive followings all because people believe and trust in who they are.

Keep Everything Active

The main thing you'll have to do with a group is to stay active.

This way people will see and hear what you have to say every day. I think it's important to do this because it creates trust and value.

When you create trust and value, you'll make sales, people will buy off you because they believe that someone who creates so much content must, know what they're doing and you do.

There are some groups that do things differently to the way I do it, but I think once you master this, you can become extremely influential and make millions in the process.

The way I do things are as follows:

Facebook Live is one way to get in front of your audience. Have a schedule for yourself, decide are you going to do this once a week, twice a week or even every day?

What you want to do here is like I said before, create trust.

It's easy enough to come up with stuff to say when you are writing it down, but when you go live, you might be wondering what to say and what to do.

How I've solved this problem is, I ask questions.

The day before or hours before you go live, ask your audience would they like to ask questions to you.

This way you can research on what they've asked and learn to teach it to them, which in turn, provides you with more knowledge.

If you really do know you're topic, you can just go live and ask your audience to ask questions on the spot.

And the best thing is that once you start a live, everyone in your group will get a notification that you're live. And when its over, you can post it to your group for everyone to watch who's missed it.

Starting out doing live if you haven't done it before can be nerve-racking. If you are nervous about it, I've set up a free "Go Live - Don't be shy" Facebook Group you can practice on.

Or, you can do what I did and set up another group for just yourself and practice to your heart's content, getting over the fear of what to say and what to do.

Before you go live, have ready a bullet list in the background, so you can work of different topics from looking at the bullet points, this way you won't get confused on what you're talking about, so less confusion for you and your audience.

Post blog posts on Group once a week. Pick a day of the week and spend the time to write roughly 1,000 to 2,000 words on your topic that you can share to your audience. Go into detail on how your niche works, share things that can actually provide results.

Use stories to help you with describing what you're talking about, make it relatable to the audience member can put themselves in your shoes. What we are building here is your image. It is important with these posts to share as much as possible, because in the future you can bundle them all together to create sellable content, deleting the posts so people can have no more access unless they purchase the book from you.

What I also think is a great way to connect with your audience is to let them know what you're up to, is to Document everything and share it to them. I do this with a "Weekly 5" which is a post I put out once a week with 5 things.

1. **In case you've missed it**
2. **What I'm doing at the moment**
3. **A tip or advice from a Blogger & Podcaster**
4. **Most popular post on This Week on Financial Freedom Forever**

5. Quote I'm pondering

Sharing these things to your audience makes it more real for them, keeps them engaged, gets them involved and shares valuable information with them. These posts, are some of the most popular posts that I produce, all because people like to see how I'm getting on.

Another way to keep your members busy would be having Polls or Q&As, which can get them answering a question that you have or getting them to pick an A or B option.

Interviewing members can be a great way to make things personal with your community and to get new members also. You could find people within your group to interview and record their story that has to do with your niche.

Then create it into a podcast, where you could share your podcast to your members to listen to and also gain new members due to having a podcast where you can invite them to join.

One of the biggest problems with running a group is Spam. Members and spammers posting affiliate links, group links, page links etc. These kinds of posts can be the death of a group and I want to show you how to solve that problem.

It's called Threads.

With threads, you can designate posts. In your pinned tab you can put short links to your threads by using hashtags. For example use hashtags that are never or rarely used like #PromotionNAMEOFYOURGROUP

To bring people to specific threads.

This really works keeping spam off the feed.

My recommended threads are:

Vlogs

Promote

Lessons

Blogs

Podcasts

Motivation

Fundays

Connect

Jobs

Etc

You can add more or less depending on what type of group you run. These examples can get you started connecting with your members.

You'll see the stats after a while which ones are working and which ones aren't.

These threads can be posted daily, weekly, monthly or random as I do.

It seems to work better for the community that I have, it might be different with yours. Test and see what works and what doesn't.

I repurpose threads and other posts by pinning them to the top or commenting on them, which will carry that post to the top of the stack so it is seen by all. This usually gets interaction with a post that has gone quiet.

That is how to keep your group active. There are loads of different tactics used by different groups. You won't know what works until you try.

Fill Your Profile With Friends

Without taking these exact steps I took Grow my community FinancialFreedomForever.org, I would not be where I am today, a mentor, a thought leader, and an influencer to thousands of entrepreneurs online.

Anyone can do what I did and grow an audience, but to have a tribe of dedicated fans, you'll need to nurture them and take care of them, to help them grow, as people and as human beings.

When using tactics like this, there are a few things that you'll need to first know.

1.) Be constant

2.) Limit to 300 a day

3.) Search Like-minded people

I grew my Community by a thousand in the first month but to grow that I grew my friend's list first.

On Facebook you can have up to 5,000 friends, you can use this to kick start either your group or your page, build a brand or grow a community. The main thing about doing this is to add friends who are as like minded as you, or that hang around the same social communities as you do.

On Facebook, there are already thousands of groups, communities and pages that people are following. These are brands, influencers, sports stars, actors, YouTubers, Instagramers etc...

You can take full advantage of this and grow your own community of like-minded people by targeting these communities and pages.

It's like this, would you rather a 100 random people that don't know what you're talking about, or 10 people that do. I know which one I'd choose.

So in order to grow your page or group, you'll need to fill your profile with like-minded people.

So, in whatever niche or topic that you are starting your business in, write down as many influencers on paper as you can. It can be as little as 10 or as high as 1000.

If you're having trouble, Google, Instagram, and Facebook can help. Just search your keyword that you are building your business on and you'll see who has the biggest followings by doing this.

Search for them on Facebook, and what you'll need to do is add them as a friend or follow them.

Join their groups, you can see what groups they are following through their profile. Connect to all these and hopefully when you are done, you'll be connected to millions of other people who have a similar mindset to you.

The same goes for not just influencers but brands and companies also. Search them out, follow them and find out where their communities are.

In these groups and pages to find the people, you want to add to your friend list, go to a comment that's on the group, page or profile that you're at.

When in a comment, click on who's actually liked the comment, then you'll have a pop up that shows a list of people you can add as a friend.

Now when you are adding friends, don't go mad, and add 1,000 at once. Be slow and consistent with it. Only add 100 to 300 a day, but not at once, split it up into two parts of your day. Facebook can be wary of people making too many friends at once and can freeze your account in a moments notice.

A lot of these people won't accept your friend request, but that's fine because you'll only want people that are active and willing to listen, these people are the perfect candidates.

Of the people that don't become friends, on your mobile phone you can go to your friend list, go to "outgoing" and "undo" your friend requests that haven't accepted you, opening extra space to invite more people.

From here, go to your group or page, whichever one you are building and start inviting people. As I said before, go slow, not too many people at once. 100 to 300 a day should be ok.

Of the people that don't join your community or page, they are still your friends on Facebook and soon enough, they will follow because, with the more people that join your community or page, you and other like-minded people that are part of your following, your page or group will be suggested to their friends and families again and again.

This is one of the ways to grow organically.

These are other ways to grow your pages like using a Viral video or a post of your own that you've boosted with Ads, and inviting the people that interacted with the video or post.

The Method I explained is Free to do, easy to implement and more targeted than a boosted post in my view.

You might say, it's a bit of a cheat, but it does work and it's the fastest and most cost-saving way to grow a community of like-minded people.

And the last thing I said, "like-minded people", is one of the most important things, because these are the people that you are going to influence, these are the people that you are going to help grow, if they didn't understand what you were talking about or teaching, it is going to take you longer to connect with them in a business manner.

One of the things I'd recommend is to only grow your community to 1,000 or 2,000 with this method because these are the golden numbers.

Once you pass 1,000 members, other people, when they do find groups or pages, will usually only join them if they have people in them.

Let your group then, grow organically, by sharing content that will be shared or even asking your members to add more of their friends.

Hold competitions, have to give aways or just ask people to invite their friends, to grow into a larger community.

This is how to grow a community of like-minded people...

Funnel Time

When starting out online there are three things you'll need before you start, the ABC...

1. An idea or a business

2. Belong to a Community

3. Copywriting

Copywriting is one of the most "important" things to learn about before you get started.

Writing styles can be different from everyone, that's the beauty of it, my thoughts and styles are mine, and mine alone and yours belong to nobody else but you.

To be a great copywriter, you don't need to be the best, heck, you don't even have to be good at spelling, the only thing that you'll have to be able to do is to tell a story.

Storytelling is the key.

There's a story about an Old Cherokee Indian, who told a tale to his grandson about the battle of two Wolfs going on inside us all. One of Evil and one of Good.

"The Evil one is anger, envy, jealousy, sorrow, regret, greed, arrogance, self-pity, guilt, resentment, inferiority, lies, false pride, superiority, and ego.

The good one is joy, peace, love, hope, serenity, humility, kindness, benevolence, empathy, generosity, truth, compassion and faith."

The curious grandson asked his old Cherokee Grandfather, "which Wolf wins the battle?"

The Old Cherokee simply replied, "the one you feed".

The moral of the story is that "whichever Wolf you feed, it will win, so choose the right one, the good one".

So, now that you know that you're going to win at this, now you'll need to learn how to write good copy.

Like I said, it's all about the story.

When you tell a story, write as if you are talking to someone face to face. Even now as I write this, I speak to you out loud. By doing this, it's like you are right in front of me. That is one of the best ways to write copy, write as if your asleep and not actually thinking. We do it every day, now do it as you're writing.

Another way to be able to write good copy is practice. When you grow your Facebook audience, practice on them, write to them as if you were speaking to them face to face.

When learning to write copy, you should read other copywriters content, write it down on paper and say it out loud as your writing.

If you do this with the best copywriters work, by writing it on paper, you'll pick up their habits. Something I've always done, even before I read about it, is to use ... after every paragraph or stand-alone sentences.

It keeps the reader, reading on...

Now, eventually, when your community is large enough, you'll want to sell them something or provide them with a lead magnet to build your email list. You can post affiliate links in your group, and sell one-off products, but you won't be collecting any information, stats or making any extra sales.

What you'll need is a Funnel, it doesn't matter what company you go with. There are a few, but the only one I will ever recommend is Click Funnels. It's far superior because of a few things.

Russell Brunson - An Entrepreneur who truly believes he will change the world. He provides 98% of his content for free so that you and I can succeed like he did many years ago when he was selling his potato gun.

Click Funnels have created hundreds of Two Comma Entrepreneurs. This shows that the system works and has integrity.

Thousands Of Training videos to help you create your first Funnel and succeed with it. These training videos are free and there's more training posted live a few times a week.

Pre-made Funnels for you to use and change to your liking. Also, Click Funnels have a marketplace where you and others can sell and sell, the best selling Funnels.

The largest funnel hacker community online. Get access "free" to thousands of other funnel hackers who what to help you, with their advice and examples.

Why Build a Funnel, because it is the greatest and fastest way to make money online.

Go check out their 14 Day Trial, and receive loads of other free goodies like a Funnel Hacker t-shirt, stickers and more...

This is my Affiliate link for the Trial. I am very thankful to you if you choose to sign up via my link.

Bit.ly/FunnelSoftware

WHAT IS A FUNNEL?

A Funnel is a system that brings you through a sales process, by first selling you something or giving you that something for free, then once bought, you are taken through a funnel of other items for sale, called upselling.

There are loads of different ways to promote a funnel to make money, you can use ads, share to a community, create your own website from it, so on.

The main thing about building a funnel is to have something of value to give your audience and when you have good copywriting, you'll get people to enter your funnel, where you'll make a ton of sales.

There are a few different types of Funnels

Webinar funnel, product funnel, fishbowl funnel etc...

Like I said, there are tons of different ways to share and make money from your funnel.

You can sell products physical or digital, like products from AliExpress, Alibaba.

Products that you make from home like art, food, ebooks, Video/MP3 recordings, courses.

Yourself for keynotes speaking, live workshops.

Affiliate links, working gigs, mentoring or even consultancy.

The list goes on...

How to find similar Funnels to take an example from for your niche?

You can take the simple step by searching the web, looking at ads that are targeting you, Instagram, Twitter and Pinterest links, but that takes time to find examples that might not fit your business model.

There is a better way to find examples that you can take from, and that is search Google. When you do, use the search term "ClickFunnels.com niche" inserting your business niche for the word "niche".

So for example, take my business model, FinancialFreedomForever.org. I did not come up with the design and layout myself, what I did was find one that was working.

Even though I didn't find my example by using the method I mentioned above, because, I was targeted on Facebook, so I took examples from it and created my own style of website.

There is a saying by the Click Funnels Community, we are Funnel Hackers, meaning we break down other working Funnels and create our own.

Something I really do not condone is someone copying other people's work. So what I do recommend is, "Copy, but don't Copy. Use the same colours, design layout, put your videos or images where they put theirs, use the same text format etc, just DO NOT COPY THEIR COPY...

You can use some similar headlines, but don't take what they have written. That is copyrighted work.

When you have found a funnel to copy from, take an example and go through their funnel to see what they provide. What's their lead magnet, their upsell, & downsell? What's the design of their funnel-like, is it clean, is it messy. Can you do something better to make it convert better...

#Tip - *"If you use the method I spoke of before about searching Google for ClickFunnels.com niche, of the Funnels you like, search their links followed by a forward slash (/) and a keyword. Sometimes you can get lucky and see the next part of their funnel without actually purchasing anything. Like when I searched for an example funnel and found one I'd like to copy, I then search that link using the keyword "FunnelExample.com/UPSELL" and most of the time it would show me the next part of their funnel, "FunnelExample.com/THANKYOU usually works also.*

To see how well a funnel is doing, head to SimilarWeb.com. Here you can search a link to see loads of different stats like, competitors, what country traffic is coming from, total visits, traffic sources like direct, referrals, social, mail and more.

It actually shows you the top websites traffic is coming from and where people are going to.

This website is incredibly handy for seeing where your competitors are spending all their ad money too.

On the website, you can see other similar websites that are similar to yours and the one you've searched. Have a look at those, take examples for each, write down key headers, start designing what's working...

Lead Magnet

Now, to get people to fall down the rabbit hole that is your funnel, you'll need a good lead magnet to give them, so they'll hand over their email to you.

Usually, the best thing to do is offer them something free, something Digital, or if a physical product that costs you nothing and them cheap shipping costs, just like I gave you this book to get you into my Funnel.

This will bring them through your funnel and get them spending their money.

I'm not trying to fool anyone, this actually works, but to get to this point you'll have to be completely honest with your audience and yourself, then they will purchase anything from you. (Be sure it's of value to them, to create a repeat customer).

It's why I feel so strongly about building a community of like-minded people, if you can put yourself on top, they will give back, it's not easy, it does take a lot of work to get there. Provide the 98% of everything you do and sell 100% or the 2% that's left.

Create yourself a "Value Ladder" for yourself and your niche, so you can earn that 2%. A value ladder is a way to structure your business to appeal your target audience.

This structure will give you something different that can offer each person that goes through your funnel.

So, use your lead magnet, offering something else on the upsell for around $10. This will get them all to pull out their wallets and spend their money and when they do, it makes it easier for them to buy the next part of your funnel

By doing this you'll be able to maximize your profit by making a different product or service options available at different payment tiers for different types of spenders.

Let's be real, some people won't go past your second or third tier right away, because they won't know you, they won't understand funnily what you're trying to provide.

That's why, I continue to say, that Community is key.

When you build up a relationship with your community, they will purchase anything from you, not just because what you are giving them, but because they will want to give back, and because they like you.

Your Very First Funnel

Now that you know what and why you need a funnel, I'm going to explain to you, on where to start and how to build one.

I recommend using Click Funnels as it's the best that's out there, you might be using a different tool, but the same main fundamentals apply with each.

It's like building a one-page website, you'll need to create it, in such a way it's going to convert viewers into followers.

Headers, keywords and design are all the main things you'll have to focus on.

Obviously, you'll need a product to sell or to give away, so that you can give your customer in exchange for their email or money.

Headers are a big thing, if you're not tugging on people's emotional strings when they read it, you've lost them, sometimes for good.

If you can't think of any on the spot, there are tools and clever ways to find example headers.

Yes, like I said before, "copy, but don't copy".

What you should be doing, and you'll hear this a lot from the top guys, is to have a copywriting file, so that you can compile a list to come back to at any given time to take examples from.

With headers, come subheaders.

The same thing applies here, use good copy to tease the viewer with the headers and then use the paragraphs to explain what it's all about.

Use bullet points, powerful imagery or video content.

Imagery and Video can show what the viewer needs.

"Look how I said "needs" and not wants", use your copywriting skills to make them need it, not just want it.

Data is what we crave as humans.

For example, would you rather follow 1 person that says he or she is doing it right, or follow someone who has millions of followers who is providing the same message saying the exact same thing.

I know which one id choose.

The one with the validation.

That's another thing that every good sales page should have, "validation" as it shows the viewer, that it is tried and tested.

Same goes for the opposite, "would you want something nobody else has, that's completely rare and precious or, something that everyone has, making it common and "accessible".

Everyone wants something that everyone else has, or something that they don't, so use these strategies to convince your customer to make the next move and provide you with either an exchange of their email or their money.

Domain

When you've purchased your domain, fix your hosting & domain forwarding toward your domain name. This gives your website more authority and makes it look authentic.

When you are creating a funnel, we'll say in this case, building one for joining your community, take examples from other websites, follow through on their Funnels so you can see what they are upselling and downselling.

Use entry into your community as your free lead magnet.

If you'd rather use something like a pdf, ebook etc, it doesn't really matter, just focus on getting them to follow through, to the next part of your funnel.

Offer them something they would find hard to refuse, always offer more than just the up-sell.

For example, your up-sell is your main product, and then add in a bunch of other stuff to make it more tasty, you know, like the shops do it, "buy one, get one free", or "buy this, and you get a years supply completely free", that kind of stuff.

"DO YOUR RESEARCH",

Don't just put anything up, look around online see what other sellers are offering, can you do better than them or can you do something different.

If they say no to your up-sell, all is not lost. Create a down-sell, something that would go well with a no answer.

Maybe they couldn't afford your up-sell, but your down-sell might be cheaper and would make more sense to them.

Maybe you have a sweeter deal to offer, add in something extra, maybe this might tickle their fancy and boost up the cost...

Test your funnel

The main thing when you've your Funnel competed, be sure to test and test again. Sometimes you might have forgotten to add in the right lead page or price of a product etc.

Even when it comes to posting your ad, be sure to go over every link on your ad, as sometimes the link could be broken and you'll end of paying for it.

It doesn't have to be perfect, it doesn't even need to be a fancy looking page. As long as you've got something the marketplace wants and needs, you'll make money.

Just get it ready and put it out there, you won't know until you try. That's why starting off with a community is a great way to test and get validation.

It can be all done here.

Ask your members to try it, ask them was it worth it and did they like the process.

When you've it tried and tested you can then sell it. You'll have validation and you'll have examples.

In your community, you can either post your funnel on the page, pin it top and invite people to come have a look.

When you are the admin of your group, every time you post, most members should get a ping that you've posted.

Even better is post a Facebook live and put your links to your funnel in the comments, as when you do a live everyone should be notified.

Don't forget the thank you page for the end of your funnel.

This can be the page to bring your customers to Facebook groups, pages, or even a new funnel, leading them down the rabbit hole.

The main thing is, just get started. You'll never know if you don't try.

(Check out Click Funnels 14-day trial at Bit.ly/FunnelSoftware)

Sell And Make Money

Ok, if you've taken the steps that I've explained throughout this book, you'll have now grown a large community.

Before you start to sell anything to them, make sure you've given them enough value and advice that you can.

This way you'll have created a certain relationship between you, the seller and them, the buyer.

When you do this, they'll be more inclined to purchase, anything of value from you.

To set the narrative and figure out what you can sell to them, there are a few steps that you can take to introduce them to your product, whether it's a physical or digital product. First, you'll have to figure out what to give them, what you can provide that will make their lives easier, something that will benefit them and make them into a repeat customer.

This whole book is about growing a Facebook community, but by selling something to them, you'll also create an email list.

To get them to make that move from Facebook community member to a buyer, give them what they need, not what they want.

Let me dig deeper on that.

Everyone wants things, I want things, you want things, like, I want a new car, but it doesn't mean that I'll go out and get it.

I want a yacht but I can't get it until I change the wording.

If I "need" it, I'll come up with some way or another to get it.

If I needed a car to get to a2b, I'll go get one, or find a way, to get one.

It's all about mindset, and if you can, create that situation, that mindset with your community, you'll make sales, lots of them.

So when you've set the mindset, all you need do is "Ask".

Yes, it's that simple, humans are basic creatures if something is hard to get, we think about it carefully and most of the time don't go to any effort to get it. But, if its convenient, and handed to us, we are more inclined to take it.

Depending on what your niche is, you'll have a fair idea what your community needs anyway. As I was building my community, people were Direct Messaging (DM) looking for information, and it was always the same, so that's what I created for them.

The best thing about starting an Online Business is that you don't actually have to own the product.

All you need do is, like I've mentioned before, "Make it convenient for your customer", and give it to them.

I'm a great believer in, if you want to become an Influencer, you'll need to create your own products, but to start off with and to get you on the "Path to Freedom", there are a few different options that can set you on that path.

DROPSHIPPING

Find products to dropship. It's not as hard as you think, finding products to sell has never been easier. There are so many tools (which I'll mention in the notes) that you can use to assist you on finding the right product.

Right, there are a few places to find products to drop ship depending on what you are going to do.

So, the first thing is to have an idea what you're looking for, which niche are you in, what do your customers need.

Once you have that organised, it should make things a lot easier for you.

If you want to sell t-shirts, there's a place online that you can design the tee, and ship it to your customers one product at a time, or if you wanted to sell something more technical, there's a place for that also.

If you wanted a finished product, all ready created for you, there's that also.

You've got to decide which option works best for your business.

One place I will recommend if you want to just get straight into selling something is AliExpress.

There's also Alibaba, but that's more for shipping in bulk if you want to resource and ship the product to the customer yourself. In some cases, you can find a drop shipper here, but most of the products are straight from the factory and can be damaged, I learned this lesson the hard way.

Finding a product on AliExpress can be daunting and nerve-racking as there is an endless stream of products. Remember, listen to your customer, they will tell you what they need. When you are searching for products on AliExpress, they will give you a massive list of similar product, use the tools they give, to get the best price and the best shipping costs.

I always look for free shipping and the cheapest, best product. I do this because I can sell this product very cheap to my customers, asking them to just pay for the shipping costs, and then make the money on the up-sell.

People love free stuff, and they'll see you in a good light, providing them with something Free. A good price to set shipping would be under $10, this way everyone can afford to pay and even if they don't go through your upsell, you now have them as an email subscriber in which you can set up an email funnel, to sell them something else down the line.

Now, you're probably wondering how can I find an upsell, what goes with the physical product I'm giving my customers.

The best way to do this is to use Amazon.

Amazon has all the information freely available for you to search.

Most sellers on Amazon are drop shoppers, to begin with anyway, and all their doing is finding products from the likes of Alibaba, and shipping them to Amazon to sell. You are basically doing the same thing they are, but instead of listing products on Amazon you are creating a sales funnel, in which they pay you for the product and then you purchase the item, sending it to their address, never spending your own money.

Now, when you have decided which product you're selling on AliExpress, go to Amazon and search for it.

More then 80% of the time, you'll find that same product there.

This is where it gets interesting. Now, you have a price for the product that you're giving away, so you can tell your customers on your funnel that it usually retails for "this much", and if you scroll down on the listing, you'll see a box that shows you what products, buyers usually purchase with this one.

That's your upsell!

On Amazon, it's been tried and tested, be sure the listing you're looking at, has lots of reviews and a good BSR (Best Sellers Rank), this way you'll see if it's tried, tested and making money.

AFFILIATE LINKS

Find and use Affiliate Links from the likes of Amazon, CJ and Clickbank.

Affiliate links are great, and better than a physical product because you don't even have to order the product for your customer. All you need do is share it in a meaningful way or send the customers through a funnel, collecting their email for future campaigns.

Of the ones I've mentioned, it's simple to get started, just set up an account and share the links. But in doing this, you won't collect any subscribers for your list and that's the important part.

Sending people to affiliate is easy but if you want to maximise sales, you're going to have to story tell. You can do this a few ways.

FACEBOOK LIVE

Facebook is great when it comes to doing live video, every time you go live, your audience should get a notification that you are. It's known that Facebook lives, now get more attention than a YouTube video.

A great way to maximise sales is to story tell, empathise with your customer.

Don't sell right away when you're live, instead carry them down a live video funnel, even mention a countdown or limited time only offer, then provide the link in the comments sending them to the affiliate.

I personally think and recommend to bring them through a funnel where you are collecting their email then sending them to the affiliate product.

This way you can sell them by email also.

EMAIL FUNNEL

One of the most popular ways to sell online, it's a pity that email marketers have his ruined, and sellers are getting very bad click-through rates.

But, there's still hope, if you have the right subject lines, headers and copy, you'll lead them through a process. If you've done your job right on your Community, this should be easy, as they'll know who you are and want to consume all your stuff.

This will bring up, click through rates.

IMPORTANT - Don't spam, send either a weekly or a monthly email with the information that you want them to consume.

But, once you have your email sales funnel set up, an auto campaign that you can easily create on any, email provider, then send a 5-day email campaign.

This can be longer if you want, but it's been proven that 5 days is the sweet spot.

Use your story mode, carry them through the five days and on day fourth and fifth day, sell to them.

Let them know what product helped you solve a problem and can help them also.

(This system can be used for physical, digital and affiliate products as well).

A FUNNEL

Same as the email funnel, but instead being a five-day event, sending them through a Funnel can be instant.

First, provide something of value that they need, then up-selling, and if they don't want the up-sell, you can also down-sell.

When they go through this process, and if they don't take the up-sells or down-sells, you still have their email, to send them an auto email Funnel.

On your thank you page, you can send them to where you want, whether it's a new Facebook page or another funnel.

To maximise profits, be sure to provide value first, the 98%, and then they will give you back your 2%.

If you have a huge active community, the difference could be huge, in the thousands or even the hundreds of thousands.

The third way I'd recommend and the fastest way to become influential is to

Create Your own.

Simply put, this can be done in a few ways, courses, eBooks, Books, DVD's, Video, MP3's, Private Podcast's, etc.

Selling physical products and sending people through affiliate links only does one thing, it make's the other person, brand or company successful, a known name. Becoming an influencer, you can do these things, but to truly become influential, you need to have your own thing.

If you sat down right now to think of 10 Influencer's in your life, you think of just them and not their companies.

They created, they are creators, if you want to be in the same class, you need to create. It doesn't matter which road you take, as long as you enjoy what you're doing. You can change directions to suit what you're doing as long as you have that "thing" you became successful from.

Become the creator, not the provider...

What do create, well, it depends really on you.

What do you do?

What do you hope to achieve?

Starting off, you need a lead magnet. That, like I said before can be taken from the stuff you shared on your community.

But you need something more valuable, something that can influence or train people, something that can educate or bring someone happiness.

Creating books has never been easier, there are websites that can be used to create books one by one to ship to individual customers. There are websites to list them and there are tools to create recordings of the book.

Courses are the same. You don't need super technical skills, or even video editing software. All the tools are readily available. Take your phone for example. That thing in your hand is a media device that has it all.

If you don't have space on your phone, which is a problem to have, use Facebook as your recording device. Create a simple group page with just yourself as the member and just go live, recording all the information that you want to share.

If you don't want to use funnel software, you can even use your Facebook page as your course landing page. If you need to edit videos, you can download them off Facebook onto your computer and use free tools to edit them. Then you can either upload them onto Facebook again "edited" or "YouTube" where you can keep them private for only a person with the link can see. (USE GOO.GL OR BIT.LY TO HIDE TO LINK).

With Video or DVDs, there are websites that can create your DVD and ship it to your customers.

All you have to do is send them the recordings and the artwork, which you can get created on the likes of Fiverr.com, Upwork.com or Freelancer.com

It doesn't cost that much to create a DVD, usually under $10.

MP3's & podcasts can be created simply with your recorder on your phone or even free tools like Facebook Live, on which you can edit the videos to take the sound off the video recordings.

You can also create the mp3's yourself by purchasing them from Alibaba.com, and doing the work yourself or you can use websites that do all the work for you.

If you want to keep things low cost you can upload your recordings onto the likes of Facebook or a course funnel.

But, In saying that, people like to receive physical things, they have more value for them, then a Digital one.

MENTORSHIP

Be Their Mentor. One of the main things I've learned on my journey is that you can be a mentor to everyone, but with this book, you can take advantage and that's what I don't want. Be sure to treat each and everyone in your community like they are your students and not your cash machine.

You'll have great power as you grow your community, you'll be able to bend the rules as you see fit, but like I said before to treat your community like they are your students.

If you create rules, to begin with, be sure to follow them because, if they see you bending them to your own advantage, they will try too and when you ban them, stories will spread online of your hypocrisy.

To become a great leader and mentor share with your community 98% of what you know, they'll be thankful for that. The more you give, the more you'll get back.

You are now a growing leader in your niche. Join with me and others who are building communities on Facebook, where we share what we have learned.

Follow each other's journey, see what works for us and share the knowledge that you've acquired, so we can all achieve success in anything we do.

This is the Path to Freedom...

Conclusion

The conclusion is usually for the end of something, but for this book I want it to be the beginning for you.

This is the start of something better. You can achieve great things and by implementing what you've learned through this book, you can reach levels of success that your peers have before you.

Many people give up on their first attempt when they try and start a business. A failure to them means that they lost and can't succeed, so they won try again.

They are too embarrassed and have no self-belief a trait I think that all entrepreneurs have. If you don't have self-belief, no one else will believe in you.

Trust in what you're doing and always aim for something more.

It's society that's holding you back, don't listen to the negative comments only understand them.

You'll know deep inside if what you're doing is wrong. I think that being in a community of like-minded people is one of the best things to do when you are passionate about something.

Share your knowledge, learn from people that have it, and connect with each other to build relationships, these are the fundamentals of business.

If you can do these things, you'll reach higher levels of success.

The difference between you and the average person, which includes your family members and friends, is that you have woken up to what can be achieved and they are still being held back by each other.

It's what we are thought in schools, to be workers, not entrepreneurs, not people that can change lives, because if we did that, there would be fewer workers and more winners which would upset the whole system.

That is why it's always said by each entrepreneur to connect with like-minded people.

That is the whole purpose of this book and what I teach.

To come together and learn from past mistakes, so that success can be achieved no matter what. You have it in you, you have the hunger, the urge and that feeling deep inside you, it's only a matter of time...

One last thing to do, that will finish this book, is that I want you to answer yourself these three questions:

1. **Do you believe in yourself?**
2. **What is it, you hope to achieve?**
3. **Are you willing to put in the work?**

If you can answer these questions truthfully, you are on the right track.

I hope to meet you someday, where I can learn from you, on what you achieved.

Never give up.

And always be good...

Daniel Mac Sweeney

About The Author

Daniel Mac Sweeney is an Entrepreneur.

Daniel runs his website DanielMacSweeney.com, where he talks about many things, mostly about the structure of business mindset, success, failure, building communities and brands, starting out online and social networks.

He is also a CEO of FinancialFreedomForever.org, where mentors such as himself, help people grow their business mindset and aim for better things for their future.

It's the #1 Facebook Community for Entrepreneurs who strive for success.

OriginalOnesies.com is an Online Store that Daniel launched back in 2015, that sells the very best and comfiest Original Onesies.

His wrote three other Books on HowToStartDomaining.com where he has a short eBook that new domainers can Learn about Domaining, from buying the right kind of name to watching Domain Sales and loads More with The Complete Step-By-Step Domaining Tutorial for Beginners.

Another one about domains DomainResourceGuide.com

A few years ago Daniel also created and developed an App for Google Play and iTunes called DaftRun – The Sports Finder. It was a way for sports people (especially runners) be able to upload, find and join events from all around the world.

He is doing a huge redevelopment and re-brand of DaftRun at the moment and it will launch when it's ready.

Helpful Links

DanielMacSweeney.com -

Read all past blog posts & weekly 5's.

HowToStartDomaining.com -

Free eBook on learning how to buy domain name property and sell for profit. The simple steps to make money online.

DomainResourseGuide.com -

In any industry, you need resources to become successful at it. In this free eBook, you'll find lots of really helpful and useful websites and tools that you'll need to buy and sell domains.

DanielMacSweeney.com/Tools -

Interesting tools that Daniel uses in his online businesses. More phenomenal tools added monthly as Daniel learns and succeeds in different industries.

FinancialFreedomForever.org/Mentor -

Hire Daniel to help you grow a like-minded Community that will purchase anything from you. Daniel will give you his time and expertise on growing a community, creating products, landing pages and make you into a mentor where people will look up to you and follow everything you do.

t.me/FinancialFreedomForever -

Join me Daniel and others in the community on Telegram where we can chat with each other in a messenger type of conversation, one on one with each other in a public space.